Michael PHELPS

Anything Is Possible!

by **Meish Goldish**

CONSULTANT:
Jim Bolster
Head Men's Swim Coach, Columbia University

BEARPORT PUBLISHING

New York, New York

Credits
Cover and Title Page, © AP Images/Chris Carlson; 4, © Cameron Spencer/Getty Images; 5, © Doug Mills/The New York Times/Redux; 6, © Xinhua/Zuma/ICON SMI/Newscom; 7, © AP Images/Richard Drew; 8, © Splash News and Pictures/Newscom; 9, © Doug Pensinger/Getty Images; 10, © Donald Miralle/Getty Images; 11, © Donald Miralle/Allsport/Getty Images; 12, © Splash News and Pictures/Newscom; 13, © AP Images/Doug Mills; 14, © Donald Miralle/Allsport/Getty Images; 15, © Doug Pensinger/Getty Images; 16, © Allen Kee/Wire Image/Getty Images; 17, © Yves Herman/Reuters/Landov; 18, © Stephen Shaver/Bloomberg News/Landov; 19, © Jason Reed/Reuters/Landov; 20, © AP Images/Rob Griffith; 21, © Tim Chong/Reuters/Landov; 22, © Roger L. Wollenberg/UPI/Landov; 23, © Heinz Kluetmeier/Sports Illustrated/Getty Images; 24, © Ezra Shaw/Getty Images; 25, © Carl De Souza/AFP/Getty Images; 26, © Jason Reed/Reuters/Landov; 27, © Simon Bruty/Sports Illustrated/Getty Images.

Publisher: Kenn Goin
Editorial Director: Adam Siegel
Creative Director: Spencer Brinker
Photo Researcher: Omni-Photo Communications, Inc.

Library of Congress Cataloging-in-Publication Data

Goldish, Meish.
  Michael Phelps : anything is possible / by Meish Goldish.
      p. cm.
  Includes bibliographical references and index.
  ISBN-13: 978-1-59716-855-7 (library binding)
  ISBN-10: 1-59716-855-6 (library binding)
  1. Phelps, Michael, 1985—Juvenile literature. 2. Swimmers—United States—Biography—Juvenile literature. 3. Olympics—Juvenile literature. I. Title.

  GV838.P54G65 2009
  797.2'1092—dc22

For more information, write to Bearport Publishing Company, Inc., 101 Fifth Avenue, Suite 6R, New York, New York 10003. Printed in the United States of America in North Mankato, Minnesota.

102009
091709CG

10 9 8 7 6 5 4 3

Table of Contents

The 2008 Beijing Olympics

Michael Phelps shot through the water like a bullet through the air. If the U.S. Olympic swim team won this 4 x 100-meter medley **relay**, Michael would get another gold medal. He had already won seven. Another one would break American swimmer Mark Spitz's 1972 record. Spitz had won seven gold medals—the most ever at a single Olympics.

Michael cut through the water with amazing speed in his part of the relay race.

When Michael began his **leg** of the relay race, however, his team was behind. Swimmers from Japan and Australia were in the lead. Michael fought extra hard to catch up. Could he swim fast enough for his team to take the lead and win?

Michael, middle, swimming the third leg of the 4 x 100-meter medley relay race

In an Olympic relay, each member of the winning team receives a gold medal. However, the win counts as only one gold medal for the country that the athletes represent.

A Rough Start

Michael was no stranger to tough challenges. At age two, he nearly died of a serious blood **infection**. He barely reached the hospital in time to be saved. Then, when he was nine, his parents got divorced. After that, he didn't see his dad so often. He lived with his mom, Debbie, and his two older sisters, Hilary and Whitney, in a suburb of Baltimore, Maryland.

From the time he was little, Michael's mom (center) and his sisters, Whitney (left) and Hilary (right), have been his biggest fans. Here they are shown watching him swim the 4 x 100-meter medley relay in Beijing, 2008.

In school, Michael also had some difficult times. He couldn't sit still or be quiet. He was eventually found to have **attention-deficit hyperactivity disorder** (ADHD). When he was nine, one teacher told his mom, "Your son will never be able to focus on anything." Yet Debbie—a teacher herself—wasn't so sure. She thought Michael could learn to focus. He just needed an activity to use up some of his wild energy.

Michael's mom often speaks for a group, called ADHD Moms, that helps parents learn how to deal with ADHD kids.

About two million elementary school children in the United States suffer from ADHD.

In the Water

As it turned out, Michael's mom had already found a great outlet for her son's energy—swimming. When Michael had begun swimming lessons at age seven, however, things hadn't gone well at first. He was afraid to put his face underwater. Until Michael felt safe, his swim teacher, Miss Cathy, let him float on his back. Soon, however, Michael learned to do more than float. He could also do a good **backstroke**.

A young Michael at the pool

At age 11, Michael joined the North Baltimore **Aquatic** Club, where he met Bob Bowman, the club's swim coach. Right away, Bowman began to study the way Michael moved in the pool. He saw how he pulled his long, thin body through the water. The coach told Michael's mom that he could become a great swimmer.

Coach Bowman (left) has been with Michael (right, shown wearing a North Baltimore Aquatic Club cap) since the very beginning of his swimming career.

Michael was such a good swimmer that Bowman made him train alongside 18-year-olds.

Getting Better

Michael trained with Bowman for hours each day, increasing his speed and strength dramatically. The harder Michael worked, the more **competitive** he became. When he was 12, for example, he lost a race and angrily threw down his goggles. Bowman got very upset and told him never to behave that way again. The coach was teaching Michael an important lesson—temper tantrums never help an athlete perform better.

By age 15, Michael had learned to control his temper at competitions.

All of Michael's training was paying off! At the Spring Nationals in Federal Way, Washington, in the year 2000, he set a record for his age group in the 200-meter **butterfly** and the **individual medley**. Michael was starting to make a name for himself in the world of swimming.

Michael's speed as a swimmer earned him the nickname "The Baltimore Bullet."

The butterfly became Michael's best swimming stroke, as he proved at the 2000 Spring Nationals.

The 2000 Sydney Olympics

Michael returned home to Baltimore after the Spring Nationals. His mom had put up a large "Congratulations!" sign in the front yard. When Bowman saw it, however, he insisted it come down. He felt Michael should focus on the future, not the past. Michael understood. "You just have to keep going," he said.

Michael grew up in this house in a suburb of Baltimore, Maryland.

Michael did, of course, keep going. At 15, he earned a place on the U.S. Olympic swim team and went to the 2000 Summer Olympic Games in Sydney, Australia. Michael swam in only one race—the 200-meter butterfly. He placed fifth—not bad for a teenager in his first Olympic try!

Michael resting at the end of his race in Sydney

Michael, at age 15, was the youngest male to compete on a U.S. Olympic team in 68 years.

Breaking Records

After the 2000 Olympics, Michael continued to practice hard. He swam up to nine miles (14 km) a day, seven days a week. He entered more swim meets, winning many races doing the butterfly. He also won races swimming the backstroke, **breaststroke**, and **freestyle**.

At the 2001 Spring Nationals in Austin, Texas, Michael set a world record for the 200-meter butterfly. Only 15 at the time, he was the youngest swimmer ever to set a world record.

Then, in 2003, Michael made history. He won five races in a national meet held in Maryland. Before the meet, Bowman offered to shave his head if Michael could break his previous speed record. Soon Bowman was bald!

Michael was now one of the top swimmers in the world. He vowed to keep on going—to the 2004 Summer Olympics in Athens, Greece.

Coach Bowman (right) shaved his hair off soon after Michael set a new swim record at the 2003 Nationals in College Park, Maryland.

The 2004 Athens Olympics

Michael thrilled everyone who watched him in Athens. He won six gold and two bronze medals. However, he failed to tie Mark Spitz's record of seven gold medals in a single Olympics. Even so, his performance was amazing. Yet what he did for a friend there was even more amazing.

In Athens, Michael (right) won the gold medal for the 100-meter butterfly. He's shown hugging teamate Ian Crocker (left), who came in second in the race and won the silver medal.

Michael could have swum in the final Olympic relay race, the 4 x 100-meter medley relay. Instead, he gave up his spot to teammate Ian Crocker. It was Ian's last chance to win a gold medal at the games. Michael wanted him to have that chance. In the end, the U.S. team won, and Ian got his gold.

Michael (left) and teammate Ian Crocker (right) with their medals for the 100-meter butterfly.

Michael ended up winning a gold medal in the final Olympic relay—even without swimming—since he had swum in the relay **preliminary**.

Helping Others

Michael helped more than just his teammate. After the 2004 Olympics, he aided swimmers across the country. He **cofounded** a program called Swim with the Stars to encourage people to take up swimming. Michael and other top swimmers traveled to many cities to speak at schools and pools. They gave swimming tips and encouragement both to kids and adults.

Michael likes to help young swimmers in his free time.

In the fall of 2004, after the Olympics, Michael started college. He went to the University of Michigan, where Bowman had become the swim coach. Michael couldn't join the school's swim team, however, since he had made money as a **professional** athlete. Instead, he helped Bowman coach the team.

After the 2004 Olympics, a street near Michael's high school was named for him.

As a teenager, Michael signed a high-paying contract to **endorse** Speedo bathing suits. Speedo agreed to pay him $1 million more than his contract called for if he ever tied Mark Spitz's gold-medal record.

Bad to Good

During college, Michael continued to compete in races such as the 2007 World Championships in Melbourne, Australia. He set five world records there.

Then, in October of 2007, he had an accident. He was in Michigan, training for the Beijing (*bay*-JING) Olympics. One freezing day, he slipped on ice and broke his right wrist when he fell. "It's over. I'm finished," he told his coach.

Michael set five world records at the 2007 World Championships in Australia.

Michael's long, **streamlined** body shape helps him move fast in the water. His large hands act like paddles. His big feet—size 14 shoes—work like flippers.

Bowman insisted that Michael keep swimming. He would have to use a **kickboard**, however, so his wrist could heal.

For months, Michael worked super-hard. Soon he discovered that something that seemed bad at first had helped him become a better athlete. His wrist had healed and his legs were now extra-strong from all the kicking.

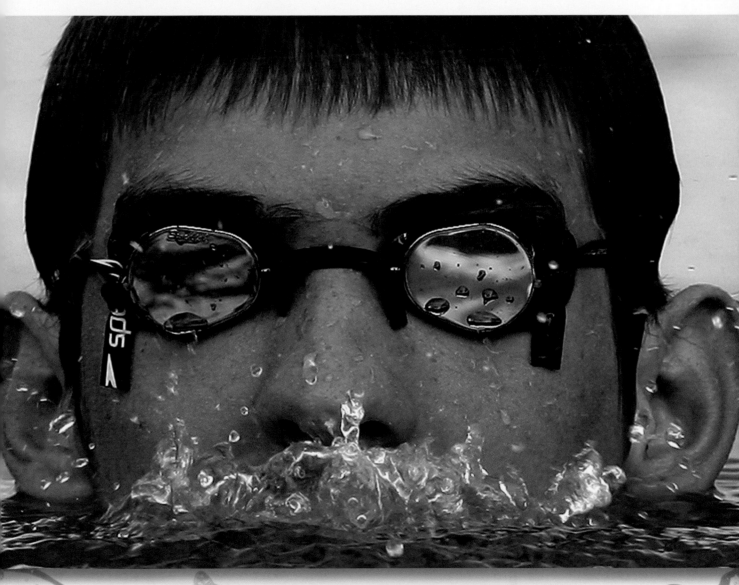

Michael, shown here at a training session before the 2008 Beijing Olympics, trained every day—even holidays—for five years before Beijing!

China 2008

All eyes were on Michael at the 2008 Olympics in Beijing. In his first six races he won six gold medals. During one of those races, the 200-meter butterfly, his goggles filled with water—keeping him from seeing. Still, he won!

Michael won the fourth race, the 200-meter butterfly, swimming blind, after water filled his leaky goggles.

By the seventh race, however, Michael was beginning to feel tired. He trailed the lead swimmer most of the way. Then, with just 20 feet (6 m) to go, he kicked extra-hard. Michael won the race by 1/100 of a second and got his seventh gold medal in Beijing. He had tied Mark Spitz's record. Now, could he break it?

Michael (left) barely beat Milorad Cavic (right) of Serbia in the 100-meter butterfly.

Michael's seventh race in Beijing was a 100-meter butterfly. His time of 50.58 seconds set a new Olympic record for the event.

The Final Race in Beijing

An eighth gold medal depended on Michael and three teammates winning the final race—the 4 x 100-meter medley relay. Halfway through the race, however, the American team was behind. Then it was Michael's turn to swim. He exploded into the water, arms whirling like a machine, and quickly shot to the lead.

Michael passed the other swimmers with his butterfly stroke.

As Michael finished his part of the race, teammate Jason Lezak dove into the pool. He rushed to the finish wall, beating the nearest swimmer by less than a second. The U.S. team had won! Michael got his eighth gold medal—at last breaking Mark Spitz's record!

Michael (right) and teammates Brendan Hansen (left) and Aaron Peirsol (center) cannot contain their excitement after Jason Lezak brings victory to the U.S. swim team.

After winning his eighth Olympic gold medal at Beijing, Michael said, "Records are always made to be broken, no matter what they are."

A World Hero

Michael went to Beijing a hopeful swimmer and left a hero—having set seven world records. People called him, at age 23, the greatest Olympic athlete ever. He had also shown the world how well a kid with ADHD could focus and succeed.

Michael gets a kiss from his mom after winning an eighth Olympic gold medal in Beijing.

Michael's success has been solidly built on skill, talent, and especially a great attitude. After his seventh gold medal, for example, he said, "If you dream as big as you can dream, anything is possible." Now Michael is dreaming of the 2012 Olympics. What new records might he set there? Anything is possible!

Michael on the cover of Sports Illustrated, *with his eight gold medals from the Beijing Olympics*

Michael currently holds the record for the most gold medals ever won by an Olympic athlete. He has a total of 14.

Just the Facts

■ Michael is 6 feet 4 inches (1.93 m) tall. His arms, stretched wide, span even farther—more than 6 feet, 5 inches (1.96 m) from hand tip to hand tip. His long arms and body help him move quickly in the water.

■ Before a meet, Michael swims his practice laps. Then he listens to rap music for 30 minutes before each race. The music helps him to focus on his goals.

Timeline

Here are some important events in Michael Phelps's life.

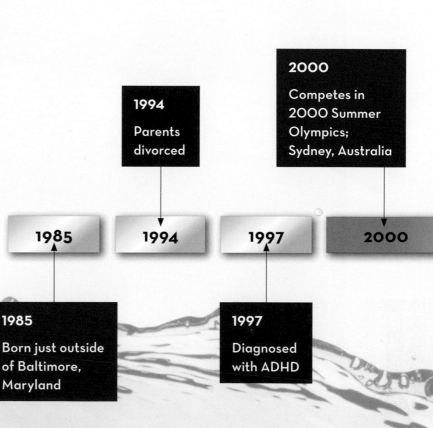

1994
Parents divorced

2000
Competes in 2000 Summer Olympics; Sydney, Australia

1985

1994

1997

2000

1985
Born just outside of Baltimore, Maryland

1997
Diagnosed with ADHD

28

■ Michael makes about $5 million a year endorsing products that include Speedo, Kellogg's, and PowerBar.

■ Michael eats up to 10,000 calories a day when training. That's six times the amount for an average adult. His typical breakfast includes eggs, French toast, cereal, and chocolate chip pancakes.

■ In August 2008, Michael set up the Michael Phelps Foundation with the $1 million bonus from Speedo for beating Spitz's record. The goal of the foundation is to inspire other young people to achieve their dreams by helping them learn to set and achieve goals.

2003
July: Sets five world records at the World Championships; Barcelona, Spain

2004
Wins six gold medals at 2004 Summer Olympics; Athens, Greece

2007
Sets five world records at the World Championships; Melbourne, Australia

2002   2004   2006   2008

2001
Becomes youngest male swimmer ever to set a world record

2003
August: Wins five national titles at the U.S. Summer Nationals; College Park, Maryland

2008
Wins eight gold medals at 2008 Summer Olympics; Beijing, China

Glossary

aquatic (uh-KWOT-ik) water

attention-deficit hyperactivity disorder (uh-TEN-shuhn-DEF-uh-sit *hye*-pur-ak-TIV-uh-tee diss-OR-dur) a condition in which people have a hard time controlling their behavior or paying attention

backstroke (BAK-*strohk*) a swimming style done while lying on one's back

breaststroke (BREST-*strohk*) a facedown swimming style in which the arms extend straight overhead, then press down through the water as they fan out to the sides and then sweep inward into a palms-together position at the chest; the movement is repeated

butterfly (BUHT-ur-flye) a facedown swimming style in which the arms make a motion that looks like the movement of a butterfly's wings

cofounded (koh-FOUND-id) started an organization with others

competitive (kuhm-PET-uh-tiv) eager to win

endorse (en-DORSS) to support or approve something

freestyle (FREE-*stile*) any kind of swimming other than the breaststroke, butterfly, or backstroke

individual medley (*in*-duh-VIJ-oo-uhl MED-lee) a race in which each swimmer swims four different kinds of strokes in the following order: butterfly, backstroke, breaststroke, freestyle

infection (in-FEK-shuhn) an illness caused by germs

kickboard (KIK-*bord*) a lightweight board that supports the upper body while the swimmer kicks

leg (LEG) part

preliminary (pri-LIM-uh-*ner*-ee) a contest held before the main one

professional (pruh-FESH-uh-nuhl) making money by doing something as a job that other people do for fun

relay (REE-lay) a team race in which each member of the team takes part, one member at a time

streamlined (STREEM-lyend) shaped to move easily through the water

Bibliography

McMullen, Paul. *Amazing Pace: The Story of Olympic Champion Michael Phelps from Sydney to Athens to Beijing.* New York: Rodale (2006).

Phelps, Michael, with Brian Cazeneuve. *Michael Phelps: Beneath the Surface.* Champaign, IL: Sports Publishing LLC (2004).

USA Today. *Michael Phelps: The World's Greatest Olympian.* Chicago: Triumph Books (2008).

Read More

Ballheimer, David, and Chris Oxlade. *Olympics.* New York: DK (2005).

Macy, Sue. *Swifter, Higher, Stronger: A Photographic History of the Summer Olympics.* Washington, D.C.: National Geographic Children's Books (2008).

Sapet, Kerrily. *Michael Phelps (Xtreme Athletes).* Greensboro, NC: Morgan Reynolds Publishing (2008).

Zuehlke, Jeffrey. *Michael Phelps (Amazing Athletes).* Minneapolis, MN: First Avenue Editions (2009).

Learn More Online

To learn more about Michael Phelps, visit
www.bearportpublishing.com/SuperAthletes

Index

About the Author

MEISH GOLDISH has written more than
100 books for children. He lives in Brooklyn, New York.
He has no gold medals but many Goldish medals.